Uppers:
Stimulant Abuse

Corona Brezina

rosen publishing's
rosen central®

New York

613.8
Bre

Published in 2008 by The Rosen Publishing Group, Inc.
29 East 21st Street, New York, NY 10010

Library of Congress Cataloging-in-Publication Data

Brezina, Corona.
Uppers: stimulant abuse / Corona Brezina. — 1st ed.
      p. cm. — (Incredibly disgusting drugs)
Includes bibliographical references and index.
ISBN-13: 978-1-4042-1956-4 (library binding)
ISBN-10: 1-4042-1956-0 (library binding)
1. Drug abuse. 2. Stimulants. I. Title.
HV5801.B683 2008
613.8'4—dc22

                                                              2007006367

Manufactured in China

Contents

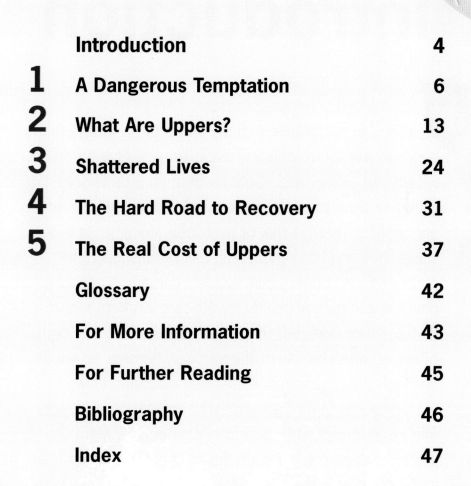

Introduction

Uppers, or stimulants, include some of the drugs that can truly devastate people's lives. Uppers give the user a sense of energy and euphoria, though effects vary from one drug to another. Cocaine and amphetamines are uppers. There is risk of overdose any time an individual uses an upper and a high risk of addiction after continued use. Uppers can severely damage a person's physical and mental health. Health-care workers report that a patient addicted to methamphetamines, one type of upper, often has all of the same symptoms as someone with the psychological disorder schizophrenia.

Characters in movies and TV shows often use uppers and other drugs without any consequence. Many celebrities and public figures have admitted to drug use at some point in their lives. Uppers are part of the social landscape—about a quarter of young people say that it would be fairly easy to get them.

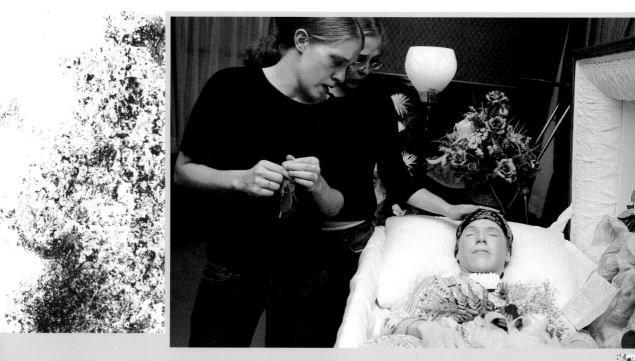

Uppers can pose a danger to drug users and anyone around them. In 2004, Tiffany Faulk was bludgeoned to death by her boyfriend, who was high on crystal meth.

However, many public-service campaigns don't work when they simply tell kids to "just say no" to drugs, using scare tactics to stress the worst-case scenarios of drug use. This type of approach doesn't help people sort the truth about drugs from the information spread by friends or the Internet. In most cases, solid information on the effects and costs of abuse should be shocking enough to convince curious teens that the dangers of uppers are very real. This is what we'll cover in this book.

1

A
Dangerous
Temptation

Every year, the U.S. Department of Health and Human Services releases a national survey on drug use and health. According to the 2005 survey, 46 percent of Americans over the age of twelve had used a drug—which includes nonmedical use of prescription drugs—in their lifetime. Pertaining to uppers, 13.8 percent had used cocaine or crack, 4.7 percent had used ecstasy, and 7.8 percent had used other stimulants such as methamphetamines. On average, people had tried uppers for the first time at the age of nineteen or twenty. About 8.1 percent of respondents had used drugs in the previous month.

The survey showed that drug use was most popular among young people: the highest rates were among people between the ages of sixteen and twenty-five. There were 2.1 million youths between the ages of twelve and seventeen who needed treatment for an

Pure cocaine is a crystalline white powder. Most cocaine sold on the street is diluted with cheaper substances like cornstarch or talcum powder.

illicit drug or alcohol problem, but fewer than 200,000 actually received treatment.

The survey dispels some commonly held beliefs about drug users—for example, 74.8 percent of drug users were employed—while confirming others: adults on parole from prison were more than three times likelier than the general population to have used drugs.

Another annual survey, the Monitoring the Future study administered by the University of Michigan, tracks national trends of drug use and attitudes among young people. According to the 2006 survey, 48.2 percent of all high school seniors had tried a drug at least once in their lives. Of the high school seniors who had used illegal stimulants, 12.4 percent had tried amphetamines, 8.5 percent had tried cocaine, 6.5 percent had tried ecstasy, and 2.2 percent had tried PCP. Overall, drug use by teenagers has declined during the past decade.

Drug Paraphernalia

The fast-food restaurant McDonald's used to provide customers with coffee stirrers but discontinued the practice after they became popular with drug users who used them to snort cocaine.

Illegal Drugs

A drug is any chemical substance that is used to change how the body or mind works. This includes a wide variety of substances, ranging from caffeine and alcohol to herbal supplements, prescription medications, and illegal drugs. Most drugs, legal or illegal, can be toxic if taken in extremely high doses.

Many drugs that are illegal today were first developed for medical use and then later restricted once it became clear that they were dangerous. An illegal drug is generally one considered to be a danger to the user, to others, and to society. Illegal drugs are categorized as either Schedule I controlled substances, considered to have no medical value, or Schedule II controlled substances, which may have some true medical use. Both categories have a very high potential for abuse.

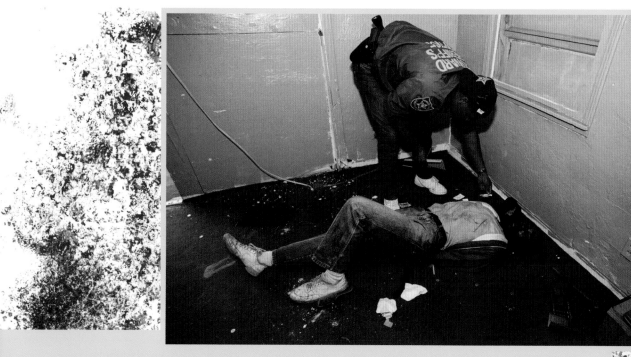

A drug conviction can result in prison time and a damaging criminal record. Here, a deputy police officer arrests a suspected drug offender in Hollywood, Florida.

Most illegal stimulants are Schedule II controlled substances. Cocaine and amphetamines, for example, are dangerous and very addictive, but they do have medical value under some circumstances.

Drug use of any kind is likely to cause some sort of controversy. Some individuals and organizations even disapprove the use of the stimulant caffeine. Others argue for tighter control of such seemingly harmless drugs as herbal supplements. When a prescription drug is found to have dangerous side effects, the matter of its safety often ends up in court.

Illegal drugs are the most controversial of all. There is disagreement on every aspect of drug regulation, hazards posed by illegal drugs, and dealing with drug offenders.

Illegal drugs fall into four main categories: opiates/opioids, hallucinogens, depressants, and stimulants. Opiates are derived from opium, while opioids are synthetic drugs with chemical structures and properties resembling opiates. Both produce feelings of euphoria and utter relaxation. Hallucinogens alter people's thinking, mood, and sensory perception. Depressants ("downers") inhibit the central nervous system, while stimulants ("uppers") excite activity of the brain and central nervous system.

The Lure of Uppers

The harmful effects of uppers are well known. The media regularly report on drug-related trends, crimes, and tragedies. Statistics show over and over that drug abuse places a high cost on individuals, families, and communities. Why, then, are so many people tempted to experiment with drugs?

For teens, the use of uppers often begins with friends. You are more likely to try uppers if your friends are doing it. Some drugs, such as ecstasy, help people loosen up around others, though the aftereffects often cause the user to feel depressed and drained of energy.

Teens, in particular, tend to be open to new experiences, even risky behaviors such as drug use. Experimentation with uppers might seem like a new way to have fun and take a time-out from everyday life. A teen's

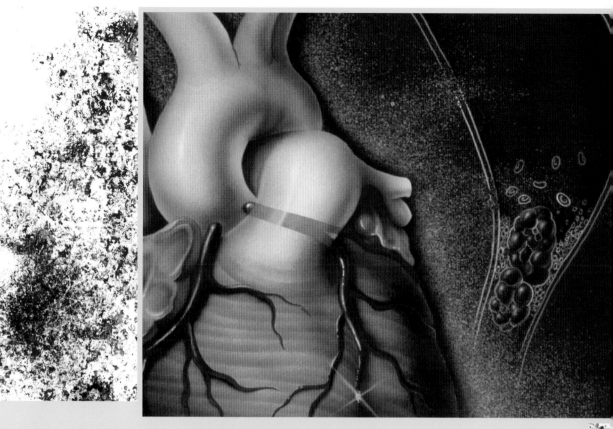

Since cocaine causes constriction of the blood vessels, long-term cocaine abuse can lead to many problems resulting from reduced blood flow to the heart muscle.

specific reasons for trying uppers may be his or her misunderstanding of the dangers involved—for example, when drugs mistakenly are used to increase physical strength or relieve stress.

Sometimes, use of uppers might indicate that a person is struggling with emotional or psychiatric problems. When someone uses illegal uppers in an attempt to relieve feelings such as anxiety or depression, he or she is self-medicating. A mental-health professional can help a person in this situation deal with drug abuse as well as the underlying causes.

Still, a majority of people stay away from uppers. What factors successfully prevent people from experimenting with these disgusting drugs? For many, it's enough that many uppers are illegal. They respect the law or fear the legal consequences of being caught. Those who are educated about drugs may be turned off by the possible negative effects: overdose, addiction, and health consequences, both immediate and long-term. If someone's circle of peers and family all shun drug use, he or she is likely to share the same values and stay away from drugs.

2

What Are
Uppers?

Stimulants generally are used to give a person feelings of euphoria, alertness, and energy. Someone under the influence of a stimulant is often confident, talkative, and outgoing. Uppers also trigger the "flight-or-fight" response in the body that occurs during emergencies. Heart rate and blood pressure increase, and the pupils of the eyes become dilated. After the effects of the drug wear off, the user is left feeling listless, depressed, and physically drained.

Amphetamines

Amphetamines ("speed") are a family of man-made uppers. Amphetamine was discovered in Germany in 1887, but it was little known until a pharmaceutical company marketed it as Benzedrine in 1932. Benzedrine was a nasal inhaler intended to treat asthma that delivered a rush of euphoria to users.

In Manila, Philippines, a chemist examines chemicals and lab equipment seized during the raid of a warehouse. The materials could have been used to produce methamphetamine.

Various preparations of amphetamine quickly became widely popular. A purified form, dexamphetamine, was found to be stronger than amphetamine, and another closely related drug, methamphetamine, was more powerful still. During World War II, both sides handed out amphetamine pills to soldiers in order to boost their energy and alertness. After the war ended, it gained a new popularity as an appetite suppressant for people who wanted to lose weight.

The United States now considers amphetamines and methamphetamine to be Schedule II controlled substances. Still, amphetamines have remained popular over the years, especially among truck drivers, students, and members of the military. Methamphetamine ("meth") can easily be made, and in the past few years, an increase in small-scale meth production in home labs has attracted considerable attention.

Amphetamines can be smoked, snorted, swallowed, or injected. The user feels a sense of elation and pleasure accompanied by increased strength, energy, confidence, and alertness. The effect can last from eight to twenty-four hours, and it is followed by severe tiredness, weakness, and depression. Using too much of this stuff often leads to aggressive outbursts, paranoia, psychosis, and severe physical deterioration. Amphetamines are very addictive.

Cocaine

Cocaine is one of the most popular illegal drugs in the United States. Cocaine users come from every level of society: powerful entertainment figures and politicians have admitted to cocaine use.

Cocaine is made from the leaves of the coca bush. For thousands of years, natives of parts of South America have chewed the leaves or brewed coca tea for a mild stimulating effect. In the nineteenth century, it was discovered that coca could be refined to make cocaine, the chemical in coca that makes the user high. Cocaine was incorporated into many medicines and beverages. Until 1903, Coca-Cola even contained cocaine. Doctors still administer cocaine in some medical procedures.

Users generally take cocaine by snorting the powdered form, though it also can be dissolved and injected. Cocaine can be further refined into more potent forms called freebase and the more common crack cocaine, which are smoked.

Cocaine gives users a clear mind and an overpowering feeling of well-being and exhilaration. The high is often immediate but usually lasts less than an hour. Afterward, the user suffers a painful coming-down period where he or she feels panicky, exhausted, and depressed.

You can overdose on cocaine by using even the smallest amounts. An overdose can raise a person's heart rate and lead to seizures, followed by heart attack, respiratory failure, stroke, or brain hemorrhage. Any of these are likely to lead to coma or death. Mixing cocaine use with alcohol or other drugs increases the chances of an overdose.

Long-term cocaine use can have severe physical and psychological consequences. A telltale sign of cocaine use is the runny "cocaine nose," which may lead to holes in the septum, the barrier between the nostrils. Cocaine can cause permanent damage to the heart. People who use too much may develop what's called paranoid psychosis, in which they experience wild delusions and exhibit bizarre behavior. In extreme cases, people have bled to death after scratching at what they believe are bugs crawling under their skin. These delusions are called coke bugs.

Crack

Crack is a more purified form of cocaine. The effects of smoking crack cocaine are just like those of using regular cocaine, but much more

A crack baby is hospitalized after being born prematurely. Many illegal and illicit drugs—as well as alcohol—can cause damage to the developing fetus of a pregnant woman.

intense—and dangerous. Crack gives the user a faster effect, a shorter and more powerful high, and more severe aftereffects. Long-term use can cause a disgusting, racking cough and permanent lung damage.

Crack has the reputation of being one of the most dangerous illegal drugs. It received a lot of attention during the "crack epidemic" of the late 1980s, when abuse soared. As a result of laws passed around this time, crack offenders today are handled more harshly in the legal system than powdered cocaine offenders. At the time, it was believed that babies born to mothers who used crack—crack babies—would suffer permanent brain damage. Unfortunately, due to the publicity of crack babies, many people do not realize that cocaine causes the same type of damage to a developing fetus. Both drugs increase the likelihood of miscarriage or premature birth, can cause developmental problems, and may result in a baby already being born with a cocaine or crack addiction.

Phencyclidine (PCP)

The man-made chemical phencyclidine (PCP), or angel dust, was developed in 1926 and was briefly marketed as an anesthetic in 1957. Patients showed such bad reactions when coming out of anesthesia that medical use was discontinued. A form is still used as a horse tranquilizer.

So what is the lure of a horse tranquilizer that's been proven to be extremely dangerous to people? PCP is a very complicated drug that produces stimulant, depressant, and hallucinatory effects. Users take PCP for the feelings of simultaneous euphoria and altered consciousness. It can numb sensitivity to pain and create a sense of detachment from the rest of the world. Its effects are highly unpredictable, though, and users may appear schizophrenic and have violent outbursts.

PCP usually is smoked, though it also can be ingested, snorted, or injected. The immediate high generally last four to six hours. Severe psychiatric aftereffects produced by PCP can linger for days or even longer with extended use. Many users experience memory loss of the drug episode.

Club Drugs

"Club drugs" is a catch-all term for a handful of narcotics that gained a reputation for popularity at nightclubs, all-night parties, and other social settings. Some in this category are stimulants (ecstasy and ketamine).

The chemical name for ecstasy is methylenedioxymethamphetamine. Try saying that while you're high! The abbreviated name for this drug is MDMA. It was first made by the pharmaceutical company Merck in 1912, but it was never marketed. In the late 1970s and early 1980s, psychiatrists believed that ecstasy could be beneficial if used during psychotherapy. Although ecstasy has been categorized as a Schedule I controlled substance since 1985, some people still believe that it could have medical value despite the harm it can do to you.

Although uppers generally produce feelings of euphoria and energy, long-term heavy use can cause depression, delusions, and psychosis.

Like other stimulants, ecstasy makes the user feel euphoric, confident, and alert. Ecstasy is unique, though, in that users feel a sense of love and openness when dealing with others. The drug tends to decrease aggression and promote sociability. It is also mildly hallucinogenic.

Ecstasy is usually swallowed as a pill, and the effect lasts from two to six hours. Higher doses can cause jitters and raise body temperature and make you clench your teeth. High doses also can lead to dehydration and serious health consequences, sometimes even death. Another risk is that there's no guarantee of dosage or purity. Since ecstasy only is produced in illegal labs, many pills may be contaminated or contain other chemicals.

Ecstasy works differently on the brain than other uppers. Although long-term effects have not been fully studied, some evidence shows that ecstasy may cause permanent damage to nerve cells in the brain.

Ketamine, also known as Special K, has many of the same effects as PCP, though at a much lower intensity. Like PCP, ketamine is legally used as an animal tranquilizer.

Cathinone

Cathinone is a chemical compound that is somewhat similar to amphetamine and is found in the leaves of a small bush called khat. Although khat is not widely available in the United States, it is dangerously popular in parts of North Africa and the Middle East. Some houses have a room reserved for khat use. Users generally chew a wad of leaves for a few minutes and keep the pulpy glob tucked in the jaw.

Used this way, khat produces a mild feeling of alertness and euphoria. Cathinone, which can be ingested, smoked, snorted, or injected, is much, much stronger. An even stronger variant form, methcathinone, is very similar to methamphetamine in its effects on the user, addiction potential, and health consequences. Both cathinone and methcathinone are Schedule I controlled substances in the United States.

Other Uppers

Anyone who has drunk tea, coffee, or certain soft drinks has ingested caffeine, the most popular upper in the United States. Beverages containing mild stimulants such as caffeine are popular across the world. Black tea contains caffeine and a compound called theobromine that acts as a stimulant. In some South American countries, people drink a beverage called yerba maté that contains xanthines, which are chemically related to caffeine. Caffeine and theobromine are found in chocolate too.

Moderate amounts of these chemicals have few negative effects on most people. Large doses of caffeine can cause jitters and nausea, though, and it is possible to overdose on caffeine. Health experts are concerned that the surge in popularity of highly caffeinated energy drinks could result in increased instances of caffeine overdoses.

Another commonly used stimulant is nicotine, the chemical found in tobacco. Tobacco has significant heath risks, whether it's smoked or taken as chewing tobacco. Every cigarette a person smokes is estimated to shorten his or her life by about fourteen minutes. Imagine how much you'll shorten your life if you smoke just a few cigarettes a day.

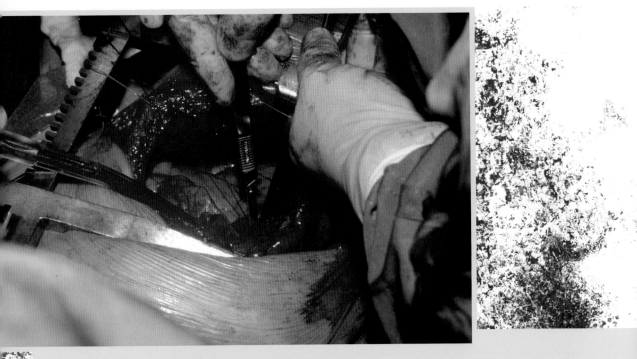

Surgeons operate on a patient's cancerous lung. Though many smokers try to quit, the strength of nicotine addiction often defeats their efforts.

The prescription drug Ritalin is a legal stimulant that helps children focus their attention and has a calming effect. It is prescribed for children and adolescents with attention-deficit/hyperactivity disorder (ADHD). Methylphenidate, the chemical compound contained in Ritalin and similar prescription drugs, closely resembles amphetamines. When taken in controlled dosages with a doctor's diagnosis, drugs such as Ritalin pose no danger. When abused as a recreational drug, however, Ritalin can produce many of the same effects and negative consequences as methamphetamine. For a more intense effect, users may crush tablets into a powder that can be snorted or dissolved and injected.

A mild amphetamine-type drug called ephedrine is legal in the United States, although sales sometimes are restricted or monitored. Ephedrine was originally derived from a Chinese plant called ma huang. It was once used in pharmaceuticals to treat respiratory conditions, but it has been largely phased out. A compound called pseudoephedrine, for example, has replaced ephedrine in many decongestants. Sales of pseudoephedrine are being restricted in some states, however, because it can be used as an ingredient in producing methamphetamine in home labs.

3
Shattered
Lives

oo many people who try uppers think, "Nothing bad can happen to me." Nobody ever expects to be the one taken to a hospital after an overdose. Nobody ever sets out to become a drug addict. When uppers abuse begins to cause problems in a person's life, it can be so overwhelming that he or she won't admit to a problem until the problem has already gone too far.

There Is No "Safe" Upper

If everyone else in a crowd has tried a particular upper without any negative effects, that probably means the drug is safe, right? Actually, the effect of uppers on any particular individual varies greatly depending on many factors. The bodies of men and women treat drugs slightly differently. The same goes for people of different ages and ethnicities. A person's health, both physical and mental, affects how he or she handles uppers. An individual might have allergies or genetic predispositions that make him or her particularly sensitive to uppers.

Another hazard of using uppers is that there's no guaranteeing the quality or purity of the drugs. Labs that make uppers don't have the same standards as pharmaceutical companies. Uppers bought illegally may be mixed with cheaper substances, or they might be different substances altogether. If cocaine powder is highly diluted with cornstarch, for example, the drug will have a weakened effect or no effect at all. If the sample has been mixed with strychnine—the chemical in rat poison—it is extremely dangerous. It's difficult and sometimes impossible to tell whether a substance is contaminated or impure, especially for inexperienced users.

Prescription uppers that are abused are also dangerous. There's a common misconception that prescription drugs aren't risky, since they're medically approved and produced by big drug companies. However, Ritalin and other prescription stimulants are only safe if they're taken in prescribed doses under a doctor's supervision. Taking these drugs on your own is considered abuse, and it can have severe consequences.

Risks of Uppers Use

If a user takes too much of an upper, the resulting overdose can cause severe illness, coma, or even death. Although the usual symptoms of an overdose vary from one drug to another, an overdose of an upper may cause an increase in heart rate, breathing rate, or blood pressure; dilated

Dangerous Combinations

According to the National Institute on Drug Abuse, cocaine taken with alcohol is the most common two-drug combination that causes drug-related deaths.

pupils; dry mouth; fever; convulsions; or coordination loss. These symptoms can lead to stroke or heart failure if not treated. Anyone who has overdosed on drugs needs immediate medical attention.

Mixing drugs—whether prescription or illegal, or combining uppers and alcohol—is extremely dangerous. The body has to deal with the side effects of two different substances that might interact chemically with each other. For example, cocaine and alcohol taken together produce a new chemical in the body. This chemical increases the effect and may be more toxic than the cocaine or alcohol by themselves. The effect of cocaine also is enhanced by combining it with nicotine, but this combination puts a greater strain on the heart. Mixing uppers with opiates—called speedballing—is a particularly deadly combination.

Intravenous drug use can have serious health consequences. Most people are aware of the danger of sharing needles with other users. This practice can transmit blood-borne diseases, such as AIDS, from one user

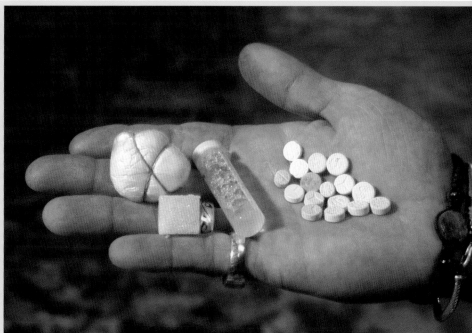

Taking uppers with other classes of drugs is particularly risky. One popular drug cocktail is called a speedball, which is cocaine mixed with a downer such as heroin or morphine.

to another who has shared the same needle. This is not the only risk of intravenous drug use, which often involves those with poor hygiene using dirty or dull needles to inject non-sterile chemicals into their blood vessels. Contamination and chronic drug use can cause infections and irritate the veins. Particles from crushed pills that fail to dissolve fully can become lodged in blood vessels and result in death.

Addiction

After a short period of uppers use, the user may learn about the most potent danger of many stimulants: addiction. A drug addict is someone who is physically or psychologically dependent on a chemical substance. The user feels compelled to continue using the drug no matter the cost or consequences, even if one of those consequences is death. This is because stimulants trigger the pleasure circuits of the brain. With extended use, the "reward system" of the brain comes to rely on the effect produced by the drug. Dependence on a drug actually causes changes in the brain. Extended use of a drug often leads to tolerance of the substance. In order to achieve the same intense effect, addicts require greater dosages of the drug.

Many uppers are highly addictive. Studies have shown that cocaine may be the most addictive of all drugs. In animal experiments, monkeys or rats with access to cocaine will repeatedly push a lever to deliver more of the drug, sometimes with fatal results. Recreational users of cocaine often will take another dose as the initial effect wears off, continuing until their supply is gone. The resulting coming-down period after such episodes is especially excruciating. After long-term use, the addict may be unable to get any pleasure out of daily life, perhaps because of changes in the brain's pathways. The drug is the only thing that relieves the condition.

The way a drug is taken affects its intensity and the chances of addiction. Snorting, smoking, or injecting a drug often produces a faster,

Animal experimentation performed in labs has confirmed the addictive qualities of many drugs and has helped scientists understand their physiological effects.

more powerful high than ingesting it. Addicts may start out by using a less potent form—dissolved methamphetamine in a drink, for example—and progress to stronger forms, such as smokable crystal meth.

Addiction to a drug results from a pattern of use that gradually develops into a habit. It begins with what seems to be harmless experimentation. The user tries a drug once or twice, perhaps out of curiosity or peer pressure. Experimentation may progress to the social stage of drug use, in which drug use is more frequent but the user still manages to keep up with daily life. Next, drug use shifts away from doing it with friends. For one reason or another, the user feels a need for the drug. Drug use now starts to affect other areas of the user's life. During the final stage of addiction, the user has a compulsive need for a drug that now is more important than anything else in his or her life. The user can no longer control cravings for uppers, and he or she will do anything necessary to obtain the drug, even if it's self-destructive or hurts others, including loved ones.

Some people are more prone to drug addiction than others. A number of factors determine how a person responds to uppers. Some evidence has shown that there may be a genetic factor to addiction, meaning that the potential for addiction may run in families.

4
The
Hard Road
to Recovery

Addiction to uppers can ravage a person's life. To an addict, nothing is as important as feeding the addiction. A sudden change in someone's personal appearance and behavior may be a sign of a drug problem. An addict might lose weight and show other physical signs of drug use, such as red eyes or lethargy. A person might suddenly lose interest in favorite activities and start hanging out with a new group of friends. He or she might start having problems at school, such as truancy, poor grades, or learning difficulties. Conflicts with family and authority figures might arise. He or she might suddenly need more money than before and may get caught stealing or lying.

An addict sometimes has to "hit bottom" before admitting to a drug problem. The change might come from receiving failing grades, overdosing, getting in an accident, or reaching some other crisis point. In some

Scary Statistics

In 2005, men were much more likely to report current illicit drug use than women (10.2 percent vs. 6.1 percent), but among young people age twelve to seventeen, the rates were much closer (10.1 percent vs. 9.7 percent).

cases, family and friends may stage an intervention in which they try to convince the addict to seek help.

Even when a user has recognized his or her dependence on a drug, the habit is extremely difficult to break. Recovery from addiction—returning to a healthy, drug-free lifestyle—is a difficult process that takes time.

Addiction to uppers is a condition that requires attention by professionals experienced in dealing with drug problems. Throughout the treatment process, it is important that the individual take advantage of any resources available to help cope. Encouragement from family and friends can be a great boost during tough times. Schools, churches, and community centers may offer support groups for people recovering from addiction. Narcotics Anonymous, for example, is the twelve-step recovery program modeled after Alcoholics Anonymous.

Treatment Programs

It's important that the uppers addict is matched with a treatment program that meets his or her needs. Abuse of uppers often goes hand-in-hand with other problems in a person's life, such as medical or psychological issues.

If a teen's drug use is caught early, an outpatient treatment program probably can resolve the problem. This usually involves a course of therapy and group sessions held after school in the afternoon or evening. For individuals with more serious uppers addictions, or for teens with behavioral issues or other complicating factors, a more intense program such as a day treatment program might be necessary.

Withdrawal from a drug can be a torturous experience. Users often feel depressed or panicked, and in some cases, they may turn violent or suicidal.

Individuals spend the day attending treatment sessions and go home in the evening. If an individual has severe problems, a residential treatment program might be the best option. Short-term residential treatment may involve a three- to six-week stay at a hospital or other treatment facility, followed by outpatient treatment. The long-term "therapeutic community" treatment model focuses on dealing with deep-rooted causes of the person's behavior. This type of program generally lasts six to twelve months.

Drug treatment begins with the user's withdrawal from the drug, which often brings about physical and mental symptoms, such as anxiety, disorientation, panic, depression, and extreme fatigue. This phase may last a few days or a few weeks. In some cases, the user will go through detoxification, the process of managing a physical dependency while clearing drugs out of the body.

With most stimulants, though, the main reason for addiction is psychological. Even after months of abstinence, such things as seeing drug paraphernalia can trigger cocaine cravings in former addicts. This is why programs tend to emphasize counseling, group therapy, and other approaches aimed at changing a person's behavior.

Long-Term Problems

A recovering drug user confronts the constant hurdle of avoiding a relapse into drug use. The temptation is particularly strong for former users of highly addictive uppers such as cocaine and methamphetamine. Treatment programs emphasize the importance of self-control and guide

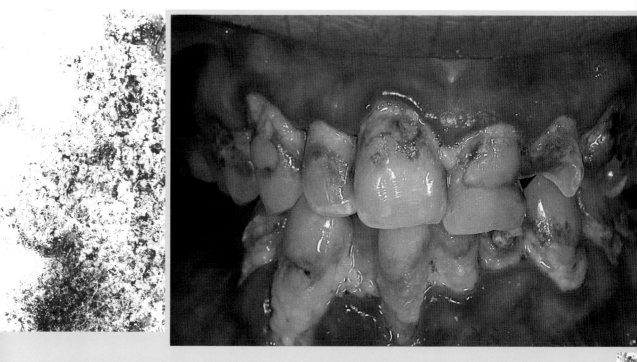

Methamphetamine use inhibits saliva production and creates conditions that can lead to the extreme case of decaying and missing teeth known as "meth mouth."

patients in ways to avoid situations that might lead to a relapse. Still, many users have trouble keeping away from uppers. Peer pressure may lead to a person returning to the drug "just one more time." Depression or difficult circumstances might sap the willpower of a recovering addict.

Even after a drug abuser has made a full recovery, physical and psychological consequences may linger. Many drug abusers are physical wrecks by the time they seek treatment. One particularly repulsive example of permanent damage is "meth mouth," the tooth loss and decay often developed by heavy methamphetamine users. Chronic abuse of some stimulants can damage the heart and the neurons in the brain. The possibility of neuron damage could be of particular concern to teens. A person's brain continues to develop until about the age of twenty. Substances that alter components of the brain could have more significant consequences for a teenage brain that's still maturing.

5

The
Real Cost
of Uppers

What is the price of a serious uppers problem? The cost goes beyond money, though an addict will go into debt and steal to keep up a habit. A recovering drug addict confronts a lot of repair work—in daily life, in relationships with friends and family, and perhaps in court. However, the global cost of the illegal use of uppers goes beyond the individual addict, who may recover one day and put his or her life back together. The far-reaching consequences are harder to fix.

Getting Back on Track

An important part of the recovery process is returning to the routines of family life, school, work, and extracurricular activities. Readjusting to everyday life can be difficult. A person might be apprehensive about returning to school after missing time. He or she will have to face peers again and catch up on class work. School life may bring a recovering user back into contact with

Here, a parolee meets with his parole officer. Even after being released from prison or drug treatment, a drug offender will be monitored for a period of time.

the circle of friends who initially introduced him or her to the drugs, and this could contribute to the temptation to relapse.

Problems with uppers can damage a person's relationship with family and friends. A drug habit can transform a person into someone that others hardly recognize. Uppers abusers often deceive and steal from those closest to them. Family members and friends may feel betrayed, and it could take time to rebuild trust.

If a person is caught with uppers, he or she will probably end up in court. Penalties for possession of cocaine, amphetamines, and other

Worldwide Business

The South American country of Colombia supplies about 90 percent of the cocaine sold in the United States. An estimated $400 million worth of cocaine is produced in Colombia every week.

stimulants are extremely harsh. Under the law, using legal uppers other than directed also constitutes drug abuse. Chances are that a teenage drug offender will end up attending court-ordered drug treatment—not a voluntary treatment program—overseen by a parole officer as well as family members and friends.

A Global Problem

The business of uppers is a problem around the world. Uppers often are smuggled into the United States from other countries. Behind the product that an American drug user buys on a street corner, there is a violent story of drug trafficking, money laundering, and "narco-terrorism." The overall consequences of drug abuse in the United States take a toll on communities, the economy, and society.

Illegal drugs have a high cost to the U.S. economy. Drug abusers drive up the cost of health care, and businesses and individuals lose productivity due to drug abuse. Drug trade and widespread drug abuse

The consequences of drug abuse and trafficking can devastate communities. This photo shows dilapidated housing in a drug-infested area of Philadelphia.

can destroy communities. The problem of drugs stifles businesses, and violence can leave residents living in a state of fear. Children, in particular, suffer when their parents become involved in drug-related activities.

Drug-related crime is a significant factor in the large number of people put in jail in the United States. In 2005, about 20 percent of prisoners in state prisons and 55 percent in federal prisons were drug offenders. In its war on drugs, the government devotes most of its resources to drug interdiction and enforcement of drug regulations. Laws require stiff penalties for violators, such as mandatory imprisonment for some drug offenses. Lesser emphasis is placed on education and treatment programs.

Drug production causes damage in another area that most people overlook: the environment. Amazon rain forests are destroyed to plant coca, and coca growers use a lot of pesticides on their crops. The chemical production of cocaine pollutes the air, water, and soil. Cocaine refinement involves three steps. First, raw coca leaves are turned into coca paste by treating them with acid and kerosene, which is dumped after the coca paste is extracted. Next, the coca paste is converted into cocaine base by treatment with a different kind of acid, a chemical called potassium permanganate, and ammonia. Again, the chemicals are released into the environment. In the final stage, coca paste is converted into cocaine hydrochloride—the final product—using acetone or ether as a solvent. The volume of toxic waste released into fragile tropical ecosystems by large-scale cocaine production can be devastating. Closer to home, small-scale labs use toxic chemicals in the production of methamphetamine, leaving behind hazardous residue even after the lab is removed.

The global drug trade poses a threat to the national security of the United States. Drug manufacturers and traffickers can build up military organizations that put a strain on the governments of drug-producing countries, often U.S. allies. These powerful individuals and organizations often support terrorist organizations.

Glossary

addiction The state in which a user is physically or psychologically dependent on a drug and feels compelled to keep taking it.

anesthetic A substance that causes loss of sensation or loss of consciousness.

euphoria A feeling of elation or well-being.

intravenous Injected directly into a blood vessel.

paraphernalia Implements used for preparing or taking drugs.

psychoactive Causing alterations in the mood or behavior by acting on the functioning of the brain.

schizophrenia A mental disorder characterized by symptoms such as delusions and withdrawal from reality.

tolerance A characteristic of certain drugs in which the effects diminish with continued use, so that the user has to take larger doses to achieve the desired effects.

tranquilizer A drug that has a sedating or relaxing effect.

withdrawal Symptoms that occur when a habitual drug user suddenly stops taking a drug.

Center for Substance Abuse Prevention

Rm. 12-105 Parklawn Building

5600 Fishers Lane

Rockville, MD 20857

(301) 443-8956

E-mail: info@samhsa.org

Web site: http://www.samhsa.gov

Drug Enforcement Administration

2401 Jefferson Davis Highway

Alexandria, VA 22301

(202) 307-1000

Web site: http://www.usdoj.gov/dea

Narcotics Anonymous

P.O. Box 9999

Van Nuys, CA 91409

(818) 773-9999

E-mail: fsmail@na.org

Web site: http://www.na.org

National Center on Addiction and Abuse at Columbia University

633 3rd Avenue, 19th floor
New York, NY 10017-6706
(212) 841-5200
Web site: http://www.casa.columbia.org

National Institute on Drug Abuse
Neuroscience Center Building
6001 Executive Boulevard
Rockville, MD 20852
(301) 443-1124
E-mail: information@lists.nida.nih.gov
Web site: http://www.nida.nih.gov

Office of National Drug Control Policy
P.O. Box 6000
Rockville, MD 20849-6000
(800) 666-3332
Web site: http://www.whitehouseedrugprolicy.gov

Web Sites
Due to the changing nature of Internet links, Rosen Publishing has developed an online list of Web sites related to the subject of this book. This site is updated regularly. Please use this link to access the list:

http://www.rosenlinks.com/idd/upaa

For Further Reading

Bayer, Linda. *Drugs, Crime, and Criminal Justice*. New York, NY: Chelsea House Publishers, 2001.

Egendorf, Laura K. *Chemical Dependency: Opposing Viewpoints*. Farmington Hills, MI: Greenhaven Press, 2003.

Hyde, Margaret O. *Drugs 101: An Overview for Teens*. Brookfield, CT: 21st Century, 2003.

Moreno, Tina, Bettie B. Youngs, and Jennifer Leigh. *A Teen's Guide to Living Drug-Free*. Deerfield Beach, FL: Health Communications, Inc., 2003.

Rodriguez, Joseph. *Juvenile*. New York, NY: powerHouse Books, 2004.

Ryan, Elizabeth A. *Straight Talk About Drugs and Alcohol*. New York, NY: Facts on File, 1996.

Walker, Pam, and Elaine Wood. *Stimulants*. Detroit, MI: Lucent Books, 2004.

Bibliography

Bureau of International Information Programs. "The Andes
  Under Siege: Environmental Consequences of the Drug
  Trade." Washington, DC. Retrieved February 9, 2007
  (http://usinfo.state.gov/products/pubs/archive/andes/
  homepage.htm).

Emmett, David, and Graeme Nice. *Understanding Street Drugs:
  A Handbook of Substance Misuse for Parents, Teachers and
  Other Professionals.* 2nd ed. Philadelphia, PA: Jessica
  Kingsley Publishers, 2006.

Gahlinger, Paul. *Illegal Drugs: A Complete Guide to Their History,
  Chemistry, Use, and Abuse.* New York, NY: Plume, 2004.

Julien, Robert M. *A Primer of Drug Action: A Concise,
  Nontechnical Guide to the Actions, Uses and Side Effects of
  Psychoactive Drugs,* 8th ed. New York, NY: W. H. Freeman
  and Company, 2000.

Kuhn, Cynthia, et. al. *Buzzed: The Straight Facts About the Most
  Used and Abused Drugs from Alcohol to Ecstasy,* 2nd ed.
  New York, NY: W. W. Norton and Company, 2003.

Kuhn, Cynthia, et. al. *Just Say Know: Talking with Kids About
  Drugs and Alcohol.* New York, NY: W. W. Norton and
  Company, 2002.

Rudgley, Richard. The Encyclopedia of Psychoactive
  Substances. New York, NY: Thomas Dunne Books, 2000.

Index

About the Author

Corona Brezina is a freelance writer working in Chicago. She has written more than a dozen titles for Rosen Publishing. Several of her previous books have also focused on topics related to science and health, including *Careers in Nanotechnology* and *Nutrition: Food Labels*.

Photo Credits

Cover, p. 1 © www.istockphotos.com/Monika Wisiniewska; cover inset, pp. 3, 42, 43, 45, 46, 47 DEA; p. 7 Shutterstock; p. 9 © Les Stone/Sygma/Corbis; p. 11 © Bryson/Custom Medical Stock Photo; p. 14 © AFP/Getty Images; p. 17 © John Griffin/The Image Works; p. 19 © Ian Jackson/Getty Images; p. 22 © Vanstrum/Custom Medical Stock Photo; p. 27 argus/Peter Arnold; p. 29 © Walter Dawn/Photo Researchers; p. 33 © David Young-Wolff/Photo Edit; p. 35 American Dental Association; p. 38 © Bob Daemmrich/The Image Works; p. 40 © Mark Ludak/The Image Works.

Designer: Les Kanturek; **Editor:** Nicholas Croce
Photo Researcher: Marty Levick